MW01245652

The Christmas Gift Of
Friendship

By Nicole Marden

The Christmas Gift of Friendship

Copyright © 2024 Nicole Marden

All rights reserved. No part of this publication may be reproduced, distributed, or transmitted in any form or by any means, including photocopying, recording, or other electronic or mechanical means without proper written permission of the author or publisher, except in the case of brief quotations embodied in critical reviews and certain other noncommercial uses permitted by copyright law.

Paperback ISBN: 979-8-9917682-1-4
Hardback ISBN: 979-8-9917682-2-1

It was a cold December night on the Forest Creek Farm. Snow gently covered the ground, and all the animals were nestled in their cozy barns. Among them was a sweet, golden-brown horse named Charlie. He loved Christmas, but this year he had a special wish.

Charlie watched as the farmer's children decorated the big, beautiful Christmas tree near the barn. They hung sparkly ornaments, twinkling lights, and placed a star on top. He wondered if they knew what he was hoping for this Christmas.

"I wish for a friend," Charlie whispered into the night. Even though he had the other animals, he longed for another horse to share his days with. He dreamed of galloping across the fields with a friend by his side.

Every day, Charlie would watch the barn doors, hoping a new horse would arrive. The other horses were older and preferred to stay in the barn during the chilly winter days. Charlie felt a little lonely and thought, Maybe Santa can help!

That night, as the snow fell softly outside, Charlie closed his eyes and made his Christmas wish. "Dear Santa," he thought, "if it's not too much, I'd really love a new friend to share Christmas with."

On Christmas Eve, something magical happened. As
the farm was quiet, and the stars twinkled brightly
in the sky, a jingling sound echoed through the air.
Charlie perked up his ears. Could it be Santa?

Charlie peered out of the barn and saw a sleigh flying high above! But just as quickly as it had appeared, it disappeared into the clouds, leaving behind a trail of glittering snowflakes. Charlie smiled. "Maybe Santa heard my wish," he thought.

The next morning, Christmas Day had arrived! The children ran to the barn, their faces lit up with excitement. As they opened the big barn doors, Charlie couldn't believe his eyes.

Standing next to the barn, tied to a red ribbon, was a beautiful, dappled gray pony. She had the softest mane and kindest eyes. Charlie's heart skipped with joy. Could this be my new friend?

The children giggled as they introduced the pony. "Her name is Star," they said, pointing to the little white star-shaped mark on her forehead. "She's here to stay, Charlie! Merry Christmas!"

Charlie trotted over to Star and nuzzled her gently.
Star neighed in return, and right then, Charlie
knew-his Christmas wish had come true.

That day, Charlie and Star galloped through the snowy fields together, their hooves leaving playful tracks behind. They played, they raced, and together, they laughed in the crisp winter air.

As the sun set and the stars twinkled in the sky once more, Charlie looked up and whispered, "Thank you, Santa, for the best Christmas gift ever."

From that Christmas forward, Charlie and Star were the best of friends, and every holiday season, they celebrated not only the joy of Christmas but the magic of friendship.

www.ingramcontent.com/pod-product-compliance
Lightning Source LLC
Chambersburg PA
CBHW042030201224
19323CB00011B/287